ALL ALONE

WRITTEN AND DIRECTED BY

X'ERNONA WOODS

"ALL ALONE"

Congratulations and welcome to a beautiful journey of self –discovery. This is your opportunity to work on enriching your life for the next 21 days. Take advantage of taking time out for yourself because it is a luxury that only you have the power to grant.

Love Always,

X'ernona Woods

"ALL ALONE"

Life is about creating new beginnings and ever -lasting experiences that support you in becoming the new you. Today you get to create your ideal lifestyle, but before you begin write three positive words that you will wear like a badge of honor.

_____

_____

_____

_____

Next you will write down three cities and countries that fit your character. It is always great to visit different places to explore a new vibe on life and what's even greater you don't have to wait.

It is when you take the time to love yourself and self- reflect you learn to become loyal to yourself, and as you build loyalty, trust, and love for yourself others will take notice. You will become a magnet for love, laughter and fun.

There are twenty-fours in a day, how are you spending your time?

Schedule Your Ideal Day   Schedule Your Realistic Day

_____

_____

_____

_____

_____

_____

_____

_____

"ALL ALONE"

Change- To give a completely different form or appearance to; transform:

The Power of Change

This exercise requires you to take a "selfie" or a picture of yourself. Place the picture directly in the center of the page. "Selfie", assignment will allow you to look at who you truly are presently and who would like to become internally and externally for the world to embrace. Focus on your best attributes and accentuate your inner and outer beauty.

What is it about you that creates your beauty?

_____
_____
_____
_____
_____
_____
_____

"ALL ALONE"

Learn to date yourself.

Having a beau is kinda sorta a big deal for some girls, but currently it is imperative that you understand the importance of dating yourself. By learning to date yourself you will learn about your likes and dislikes about yourself a very sufficient tool that will support you attracting someone suitable for you. It is quite important to learn the importance of connecting and become comfortable with who you are and what you stand for presently. And for those annoying things you dislike about yourself it provides the opportunity to change for a more enriching you.

First Step: Get appropriately dress. Not everyone is a fashionista ,but luckily you can visit an array of department stores like MACYS and many more stores who provides you will your own personal stylist for free to support you in discovering a look that works for you. Remember style is not how expensive your attire cost, but rather your confidence within yourself.

Second Step: Dine Yourself

Explore various restaurants outside your local neighborhood. Visit the array of sites that offer major deals like Groupon, Living social to name a couple and take a journey on treating your palate to foods that you wouldn't normally dare to try . Step outside your comfort zone, sometimes you have to get uncomfortable to move to the next level.

"ALL ALONE"

Relax...Relate... Release....

There are various ways to relieve stress. Unfortunately, stress is a part of life and it is better to learn how to relieve stress early on to prevent chronic illness.

Did You Know?

40% of teens report feeling irritable or angry. A third say stress makes them feel overwhelmed depressed or sad. Teen girls are more stressed than boys, just as women are more stress than men nationally.

*40% say they neglected responsibilities at home due to stress.

*21% neglect work or school due to stress

*32% experience headaches

*26% report changes in sleeping habits

*26% report snapping or being short with classmates and teammates

How do you relieve stress?

_____

_____

_____

Meditate

Sit up straight on the on the floor. Close your eyes. Place hand on your belly to connect with your breathing as you allow distracting thoughts flow away.

Breathe deeply for five minutes. Slowly inhale through your nose and exhale through your mouth.

Be Present

Focus on one behavior. For example if you are walking take time to feel the air, connect with nature etc.

Connect with others

Having a great support system is a wonderful way to manage stress.

Decompress place a warm around your neck and shoulders for ten minutes.

LOL LAUGH OUT LOUD

TURN up the radio. Play a happy song to change your vibe.

Exercise.

Release endorphins (happy hormones)

Acknowledge Your Greatness

Record your accomplishments and future goals.

Treat yourself out for a special treat.

"ALL ALONE"

Experiment or Not Experiment

The drug industry will forever exist because it provides a pseudo escape from the woes of life and provides temporary pleasure. Fortunately for you today you will you be given the opportunity to write why drugs won't work for you as you are building a strong foundation that will uplift and encourage you to truly understand that popping molly, smoking dro etc. is only a temporary fix. You will discover that you show an undeniable disconnection to your higher greater self when you take drugs that alter your inner and outer beauty. It doesn't serve as an accomplishment to the pathway you are headed upon. **Note: Contrary to popular belief …Not everyone is doing drugs!**

List ten reasons why you should not indulge in drugs

1._____

2._____

3._____

4._____

5._____

6._____

7._____

8._____

9._____

10._____

"ALL ALONE"

Idle minds leads to idle actions which equates to trouble for you.

What are you spending your time doing? Now is the time to explore great adventures, to take you from a place of doing unlawful, and take on behaviors that ultimately do not and will never will for you.

Clubs

Work

Start your own business

Fun Recreational Activities

"ALL ALONE"

FREE SUPPORT IS PRICELESS

CONTRARY to popular belief counselors, psychiatrist, psychologist or any mental health professions is not for **"crazy"** people. Unfortunately life brings a plethora of hang ups and bang ups you may find yourself in the center of those life lessons.

It is wonderful to have someone to actually listen for understanding and support you in working with life lessons. To package my words nicely... Go see your counselor!!!

I have visited countless schools where students do not utilize the counselors because of the stigma of being crazy. I think it's the opposite when you have free on hand support. Trust and BELIEVE AS YOU GET OLDER AND INEVIATBLY YOU WILL those issues as a child will come up for you in various areas of your life. An ounce of prevention is worth a pound of cure. And besides a psychologist, counselor prices range from $250 per hour and up.

"ALL ALONE"

What is your financial thermostat?

There will always be a time where you will need money.

It is important that you should make a decision on how much money you desire and what will it take in order for you to create that desired amount. Make the decision whether you want to be rich or poor. Understanding the power if decision making will support you in not hitting unfortunate financial bumps in your life.

Do you know the four things you can do with your money?

1. SAVE

2. INVEST

3. DONATE

4. SPEND

"ALL ALONE"

BE GRATEFUL....

List ten reasons why you should be grateful.

I have learned if you don't give yourself enough reasons you won't find the value and will easily disconnect from someone or something that you truly deserve to have because of your ungratefulness.

1._____

2._____

3._____

4._____

5._____

6._____

7._____

8._____

9._____

10._____

"ALL ALONE"

What is your image?

Look in the mirror 3 times a day.

Self -Reflection

How do you view yourself?

Choose five people to interview.

Name 10 reasons

Why you like who you see in the mirror.

1._____

2._____

3._____

4._____

5._____

6._____

7._____

8._____

9._____

10._____

"ALL ALONE"

The poison that lies on your tongue will inevitably cause you to be the one who is poisoned. Every day we have the opportunity to say kind words to ourselves, peers, parents, and strangers. Give an example of when you spoke negative about yourself or someone. What was the end result of speaking negatively?

_____
_____
_____
_____
_____
_____
_____
_____
_____
_____
_____
_____
_____
_____
_____
_____

"ALL ALONE"

Michelle found herself in a precarious situation that lead to her to a detrimental circumstances.

Below you will answer questions that will support you in making positive decisions that work for you.

Who is the "Kevin" in your life?

Do you know of any guy that resembles the behavior of Kevin?

How do you interact with someone like Kevin?

What are the dangers if any that you see by befriending or dating someone like Kevin?

_____

_____

_____

_____

_____

_____

Should Michelle have informed her mother, but Uncle Jeff?

_____

_____

What are some reasons why you would not tell if someone hurt you physically or mentally to a responsible adult?

_____

"ALL ALONE"

When is there an appropriate time to tell a responsible adult that someone is acting or behaving inappropriately with you?

_____

_____

_____

_____

_____

_____

_____

Michelle didn't inform her mother where she was going, have you ever deceived your parents about where you were going or who you were hanging out with?

_____

Why should you tell a responsible person where you are going and with whom? Why is it important to tell someone?

_____

_____

_____

_____

"ALL ALONE"

Why wouldn't you tell a responsible adult of your whereabouts?

_____

_____
_____
_____
_____

List five people who you have their contact information, name, number, and address who you trust. If you don't have all of their information then today is the day to gather their information.

_____

_____
_____
_____

Have you ever been in a precarious situation where you felt you had to compromise your morals to be friends with someone Example: Michelle with Kevin.

_____
_____
_____
_____

How did you feel after you compromise your judgment?

_____
_____

What was the end result of your compromise?

_____
_____
_____

"ALL ALONE"

Deservability

Repeat 3x's per Morning-Noon-Night – The more you say it the more you believe it you will achieve. I deserve. I deserve all good. Not some of it, not a little bit, but all good. I now move past all negative restricting thoughts. I release and let go of limitations of my parents. I love them, and I go beyond them. I am not their negative opinions, nor their limiting beliefs. I am not bound by fears or prejudices of the current society I live in. I no longer identify with limitation of any kind.

In my mind, I have a total freedom. I now move into a new space of consciousness, where I am willing to see myself differently. I am willing to create new thoughts about myself and about my life. My new thinking becomes experiences.

I now know and affirm that I am one with the Prospering Power of the Universe. As such , I now prosper in a number of ways. The totality of possibilities lies before me. I deserve love, an abundance of love. I deserve to live comfortably and prosper. I deserve freedom to be all I can be. I deserve more than that. I deserve good . I deserve to be the Author of my life!

"ALL ALONE"

Make Yourself Proud Everyday

List ten reason why you should be proud of yourself every day.

_____

_____

_____

"ALL ALONE"

Who do you need to be in order to be proud of yourself?

_____

_____

_____

"ALL ALONE"

Selfish=Self-care

It's okay to be selfish with your body time, and love.

When should you become selfish?

_____

_____

_____

"ALL ALONE"

Who will you become in the next two-three months, five years, ten years? What will you change about yourself?

_____
_____
_____
_____
_____
_____
_____
_____
_____
_____
_____
_____
_____
_____
_____
_____
_____
_____
_____
_____
_____
_____
_____
_____

"ALL ALONE"

The truth that is hardest to tell, should be told the loudest.

What truth about you needs to be told?

_____

_____

_____

_____

"ALL ALONE"

Disciplining yourself to do what you know is right and important although difficult is the high road to pride, sell-esteem and personal satisfaction. - Margaret Thatcher

What tactics will you take to stay focus?

_____
_____
_____
_____
_____
_____
_____
_____
_____
_____